INSIGNIFICANCE

TERRY JOHNSON

The Royal Court Writers Series
published by Methuen
in association with the Royal Court Theatre

For Kenneth Hardacre

The front cover photograph shows Michael Emil as THE PROFESSOR *and Theresa Russell as* THE ACTRESS *in the film of* INSIGNIFICANCE. *Reproduced courtesy of Glinwood Films.*

A METHUEN PAPERBACK

First published as a paperback original in 1982 by
Methuen London Ltd, 11 New Fetter Lane, London EC4P 4EE
in association with the Royal Court Theatre, Sloane Square, London SW1.
Published in the United States of America by Methuen Inc, 29 West 35th Street,
New York, NY 10001
Reprinted 1983
Second edition published 1986
Printed by Expression Printers Ltd, London N7.

Copyright © 1982 by Terry Johnson

ISBN 0 413 60240 0

Insignificance was first performed at the Royal Court Theatre, London, on 8 July 1982, with the following cast:

PROFESSOR   Ian McDiarmid
White-haired and bright-eyed. Around seventy years old.
He wears a shabby sweatshirt and a loose, dark suit.
He thinks a great deal and speaks concisely.

SENATOR   William Hootkins
A fat, red, sweaty man, wearing a large, pale,
sweaty suit.

ACTRESS   Judy Davis
A stunning blonde carefully composed to look a little
younger than she is. Listening to her one might guess at
twenty years, or at other times, forty.

BALLPLAYER   Larry Lamb
All-American boy turned forty. He resembles a
retired astronaut.

HEAVY
Tall, dark mobster type, probably CIA.

Directed by Les Waters
Designed by Tony McDonald

1953. A hotel room in New York. The room is modern, circa '53, and has a large expanse of window looking out onto the city. There are stars and there is light from a neon sign on a building below. There is a door to the corridor, one to the bathroom, and a double bed.

'I believe with Schopenhauer that one of the strongest motives that leads men to Art and Science is escape from everyday life with its painful crudity and hopeless dreariness, from the fetters of one's ever-shifting desires. With this negative motive there goes a positive one. Man tries to make for himself in the fashion that suits him best a simplified and intelligible picture of this world: he then tries to some extent to substitute this cosmos of his for the world of experience and thus to overcome it. Each makes this cosmos and its construction the pivot of his emotional life in order to find in this way the peace and security he cannot find . . .'

Albert Einstein

*A New York hotel room, 1953, night.
The* PROFESSOR *sits facing an
incongruous blackboard covered with
complex calculus. He is seventy, white
haired, bright eyed. He wears a shabby
Princeton sweatshirt and has bare feet.
Beside him is a pile of paper a foot tall. A
Gladstone bag lies on the bed. A clock is
ticking. He hears a cheer in the distance and
goes to the open window. His face is lit by
flashing red neon. He looks upwards.
There is a knock on the door.*

SENATOR (*off*): Professor?

*He goes to the door.
The* SENATOR *stands with a bottle like a
nightmare salesman. He is a fat, sweaty
man in a pale, sweaty suit.*

It's a dog of a night, Professor. I got
bourbon or I got rye. (*He steps in.*) Sort of
a peace offering for calling on you so late
but I couldn't see how you'd be sleeping
on a night like this. You'll have to forgive
my intrusion but I've got something to say
to you that's just got to be said before the
morning. This is a hell of a hotel, ain't it?
You have a good flight? Each time I fly
there is half as much time spent in the air
and twice as much spent in the terminal.
Progress! Now we got whisky and we got
the whole night ahead of us. Half the
night for you and half the night for me.

PROFESSOR: Thank you no, I don't
drink.

SENATOR: And I don't take no for an
answer, Professor. Drink! It's a dog of a
night and tomorrow's going to be a dog of
a day.

He offers a drink to the PROFESSOR,
*who takes it into the bathroom to add
water.*

PROFESSOR: Would you like some
water?

SENATOR: No sir. Did you know that
according to the law of probability you
drink a glass of water and you drink a
piece of Napoleon's crap? Perhaps even
Mussolini's but more likely Napoleon's
on account of he's been dead longer.
Attila the Hun's a dead cert, he's been
gone so long. It's pure probability you
take a glass of water you just drink a piece
of Attila the Hun's arsehole. I don't drink
water. I don't intend to be any part of the
earth's alimentary canal, I can tell you
that, no sir.

PROFESSOR: The same probability must
surely exist for all liquids.

SENATOR: Whisky's a cleanser. You ever
drop a worm in whisky? It'll go stiffer'n a
nail in two minutes. If I'm drinking pieces
of Mussolini I know they're dead pieces of
Mussolini and aren't still swimming
around with minds of their own. Now I'm
not an educated man Professor, but I'm a
jackdaw when it comes to picking up little
facts of knowledge. I like to think I could
hold my own, least ways up to the letter S.

PROFESSOR: S?

SENATOR: I make it a rule to learn one
new word a day. I'm up to midway
through the S's. Want to know today's
word? Solifluxion. You know what that
means?

PROFESSOR: The movement of soil due
to natural causes.

SENATOR: You got to W already, I bet.
Yes sir, the movement of soil due to
natural causes. I love knowledge. I'd give
a great deal to know all you know. That
the stuff you hump about with you all the
time? Must be quite a few years' work
right there. To tomorrow, Professor.
(*The* SENATOR *drinks.*) Now the first
thing you have to remember is that you
ain't on trial. You're not accused of
anything. You're not here to be accused.
If you feel accused then I'm an unhappy
man. Are you feeling accused?

PROFESSOR: No, I am feeling
persecuted.

SENATOR: Are you now?

PROFESSOR: Or have I ever been?

SENATOR: That ain't an accusation, it's
an enquiry. Entirely off the record, would
you like to tell me what your answer to
that question might be? There's only two
answers; yes or no. Those few citizens
who have decided not to use either of
those words, I'll tell you, they have
turned these hearings into one royal pain.
You know the most times one man has
cited the Fifth Amendment? Seventy-
nine times. He got awfully tired. He got to
yelling it then he got to muttering it, then
he got to repeating it so hoarse we had to

ask him to speak up four times so's we could hear what he was saying. Fourth time he just said, 'Yes, I was'. He'd meant yes all along. Now I'm not here to persuade you to one testimony or another, all I ask is that you give us a straight answer to a straight question so we can all fly home and get a long weekend. Last time I bought a ticket south I had to spend two extra sessions trying that jumped-up nigger Robeson for contempt and missed the damn plane. Try one of those little words, Yes or No, by way of experiment.

PROFESSOR: No?

SENATOR: You're not nor have you ever been?

PROFESSOR: What then?

SENATOR: We'd go for perjury.

PROFESSOR: Ahah. I've been named.

SENATOR: Three times. I came here tonight to make the situation clear. You're not a politician or a military man; you're not used to kicking about in the mud and coming up smelling of roses. I'd put you in the same category as some of the movie people we've talked to; the type of person to whom mud sticks. There's a little solifluxion going on right now; the dirt's shifting and it's heading your way. Help us and we'll help you come out clean.

PROFESSOR: To come out clean I have to answer Yes?

SENATOR: Yes would be just fine by us. Of course you'd need to couple that with a denunciation of any Communist ideals you once held. And a formal condemnation of the Soviet's arms initiative wouldn't do you any harm.

PROFESSOR: Would that be all?

SENATOR: You could show good faith and give us a few names.

PROFESSOR: Am I talking to an official representative of the House Committee for UnAmerican Activities?

SENATOR: Well, no one ever put a scare into a rabbit by pretending they haven't got a dog. Guess I'm the dog.

PROFESSOR: What if I answered yes but refused to condemn Communism or to name names, what then?

SENATOR: Shit, that what you're going to do? I'll tell you in confidence, I don't think the hearings proper are going to go on for much longer. You could be our last big fish, Professor, and what a fish. Knows all there is to know about them Photons, 'tomic structure, cosmology, Jewish problem. They call you Daddy of the H bomb and the True Child of the Universe. It's in your power to just about wrap the thing up. We need a man of stature who, when faced with frankfurters or hotdogs, chose hotdogs. Token American if you like. After all you chose America.

PROFESSOR: In my lifetime I have been accused by the Swiss of being a German Fascist, by the Germans of being a Zionist conspirator, and by the Americans of being a German Fascist, a Zionist conspirator and now a Soviet Communist. I have been both an Internationalist and a diehard patriot. By two magazines in the same week I was called a conscientious objector and a warmonger; both were reviewing a speech I made to the Mozart Appreciation Society of New England. Now I am asked to stand and say Yes or No to a question that belongs in a fourth-grade Latin examination paper. Answer Yes or No so that you can decide if I deserve to be called an American. I tell you, on or off the record, I don't care. I never chose America, to my shame I was avoiding Dachau.

SENATOR: Strange how you talk to a good Jew nowadays, that subject always comes up. Dachau. Same threat to democracy we're asking you to fight.

PROFESSOR: World War Two had nothing to do with Communism.

SENATOR: What? . . . ? Whole damn thing was a Soviet plot!

PROFESSOR: 15,000,000 dead Russians, a Soviet plot?

SENATOR: They're tricky. Ask yourself this; what's left of Europe that'll ever be a threat to the Soviets? Round one's theirs. So, what do you say?

PROFESSOR: I say you ought to see a psychiatrist. Goodnight, Senator.

SENATOR: It'd be a mighty shame if all you stood for was to get muddied up for the sake of haggling over a constitutional legality. Don't make the mistake of treating this like a freshman's debate on civil liberties; there are some who have done that and sounded just fine on the day. One guy got applauded by the fucking stenographer but he ain't earnt jack shit since. Nor has the stenographer. This thing's got the power to change your life so it's never the same again, worse than a swollen prostate. I glanced through your file. So what about a little co-operation here?

PROFESSOR: I can make it very simple. I will not, ever, testify.

SENATOR: You're subpoenaed for tomorrow.

PROFESSOR: I am here to speak at the Conference for World Peace. The date of my subpoena coincides quite beautifully but it will not prevent me from attending. Nor if I had arranged to go fishing would it have prevented me from catching fish.

SENATOR: You ignore a house committee subpoena and that may be all that's left for you to do. Must be near a lifetime's work there. I heard tell you refuse to have copies made of those, why is that? Be a tragedy if they was to go astray. (*The* SENATOR *stands.*) You're called for nine-thirty. I'll be here around eight to pick you up.

PROFESSOR: Bring a good book.

SENATOR: I have every faith in the testimony you'll give Professor. Peace Conference can slug it out in your absence. Waste of time anyway, ain't nobody going to press no button; we got too much invested; I mean think of the real estate.

The SENATOR *leaves.*
The PROFESSOR *has a thought. He avoids the thought by plunging into the calculus. He takes a new chalk.*

The lights fade.

There is a knock on the door.

The lights come up.
The PROFESSOR *has been asleep in the chair.*

PROFESSOR: Who is it?

ACTRESS (*off*): You wouldn't believe me.

He puts a stub of chalk in his pocket and opens the door. The ACTRESS *is dressed in a pleated white skirt and dark glasses, a well-worn fur coat.*

ACTRESS: Hi.

PROFESSOR: Hello.

ACTRESS: Are you busy? Only I'm being pursued.

PROFESSOR: In that case you must come in.

ACTRESS: Thank you. This is an awful liberty I know, but I'm very honoured to meet you.

PROFESSOR: Who is pursuing you?

ACTRESS: Just about everybody. I thought you'd be asleep. It's three-thirty. (*Pause.*) Would you like me to go?

PROFESSOR: No, please.

ACTRESS: I had to come and see you before you fly home or I fly west and I've hardly had a moment. I've been shooting all week. (*She removes her glasses.*) You don't recognise me do you?

PROFESSOR: Ahhhm . . . no.

ACTRESS: That's wonderful. (*Pause.*) Have I interrupted your work?

PROFESSOR: No, just some calculations.

ACTRESS: What are you trying to calculate?

PROFESSOR: I am trying to unify the fields.

ACTRESS: Will it take long?

PROFESSOR: Another four years perhaps.

ACTRESS: Gee.

PROFESSOR: You are an actress?

ACTRESS: Mmmhmm.

PROFESSOR: What is your name?

She goes to the window and points out at the flashing red neon. We cannot see the sign itself, only the light from it.

Ahah. I've heard of her. Is she good?

ACTRESS: She tries hard.

PROFESSOR: Why is she here?

ACTRESS: A visit.

PROFESSOR: Why?

ACTRESS: You're famous!

PROFESSOR: So are you.

ACTRESS: I know. We have an awful lot in common.

PROFESSOR: It's not a good reason for a visit.

ACTRESS: I know. I was being facetious.

PROFESSOR: Because of being famous everywhere I go people fall over themselves to be with me, like a troupe of clowns chasing an automobile. Because of fame everything I do is likely to develop into a ridiculous comedy.

ACTRESS: You're lucky. Everything I do develops into a nightmare. People throw themselves in front of me and I don't dare stop.

PROFESSOR: Who in particular is pursuing you at this time of night?

ACTRESS: Oh, a drama coach and an ex-baseball star, the usual kind of person. I think I lost them. Have I disturbed you?

PROFESSOR: No, no.

ACTRESS: Shall I go?

PROFESSOR: No, no, no.

There is an awkward pause.

What kind of movie are you . . .

ACTRESS: Shooting?

PROFESSOR: Shooting?

ACTRESS: A crummy one.

PROFESSOR: Who do you er, act?

ACTRESS: I play this girl. She's a what, not a who. She has no name; she's just a figment of this guy's imagination. He just imagines having me around the place, you know? I spend the entire movie in the tub or in the kitchen or having my skirt blown up around my ears. They fixed up a wind machine beneath a grating out on fifty-third; I've been out there since before midnight having my skirt blown up around my goddam ears. I know now why umbrellas give up. So it got to three-thirty and there were about a thousand people cheering each time the fan went wham and the police finally made us pack up at three so's the milk trucks could get through the crowd. And I knew my last chance to see you before you left New York or I died of intimate exposure would be to wake you up in the middle of the night and I told myself, 'Go ahead, because if he doesn't understand how you have to wake people up in the middle of the night sometimes, nobody will.' I mean if he doesn't give a damn about it then he's the sort of person worth meeting enough to take the chance he might be grouchy and tell you to get lost, and anyway, I figured I'd been making such a dodo of myself all night I couldn't make a bigger dodo of myself if I came, so I came. I thought, 'What the hell'. Have you ever noticed how 'What the hell is always the right decision? What did you do tonight?

PROFESSOR: I er – arrived and attempted to derive the tangenital vector quantities for Oc^2 when the value for t is infinity.

ACTRESS: You had a bad night too, huh?

PROFESSOR: Certainly. I could have been beneath the stars watching a pretty girl have her skirt blown up around her ears.

ACTRESS: Would you have watched?

PROFESSOR: Would you have liked me to?

ACTRESS: Yes. It would have embarrassed me. I was upset by the others but they didn't embarrass me. I don't think a girl should go through a thing like that without feeling embarrassed. It doesn't seem natural somehow.

PROFESSOR: How would I have embarrassed you if they couldn't?

ACTRESS: They saw a star doing glamorous things right there on the block, you'd have seen a girl flashing her legs for a bunch of jerks.

She leans out of the window.

Mothers!

I have to project my self-loathing onto guys who like thighs, isn't that pathetic? You never shouted out of a window, did you, except to stop your kid from falling out of the tree or something.

PROFESSOR: No, I never did.

ACTRESS: It's a cheap trick.

Pause.

Could I explain something to you?

PROFESSOR: Certainly, what?

ACTRESS: The Theory of Relativity.

PROFESSOR: All of it?

ACTRESS: Just the Specific Theory. The General Theory's a little too complex to go into here don't you think?

PROFESSOR: Just the Specific?

ACTRESS: Mmmmmm.

PROFESSOR: Because it's there?

ACTRESS: Because I'm here. Would it really bore you? I'll never have another chance to prove it.

PROFESSOR: Why should you have to prove it? You know what you know.

ACTRESS: But you don't believe me.

PROFESSOR: If you say you understand Relativity then I believe you.

ACTRESS: You're just saying that to avoid seeing me embarrass myself.

PROFESSOR: Of course not.

ACTRESS: You honestly believe I understand Relativity?

PROFESSOR: Yes.

ACTRESS: Swear to God?

PROFESSOR: Whose God?

ACTRESS: Yours.

PROFESSOR: Prove it. With my God you take no chance.

ACTRESS: I'm not theoretical, I demonstrate. I brought a few things.

She produces an array of objects from her coat pockets, things gathered for the purpose, and demonstrates the following as extravagantly as possible.

If I make a little mistake I want you to stop me. If I go completely off the rails I think you'd better let me finish. I don't always think along exactly your lines I mean who does, but I can get the same results. Eventually. That's valid isn't it? Ready?

PROFESSOR: Go.

ACTRESS: Well, first of all you have to know two things. The first thing is that if you drop a copy of *The Brothers Karamazov* in a moving train it doesn't fly backwards and flatten the conductor. It drops relative to the train. That's a very important word, please put it in your vocabulary book. So if anybody does any experiments on a moving train or in a laboratory at Princeton the results will always be the same because wherever his springs and rulers and balls are he's there too. That's the first thing you have to know. The second thing you have to know is that light absolutely always travels at the same speed in all directions. 186,282 miles per second?

PROFESSOR: .397.

ACTRESS: It got faster?

PROFESSOR: We got more accurate.

ACTRESS: Then don't confuse me. Now we have to imagine a man in a car travelling at thirty miles an hour, and a hiker standing by the road waiting for a lift. The driver, as he drives up at thirty miles an hour throws a stone at the hiker ahead of him at another thirty miles an hour. He's a league pitcher. So the question is if the car is travelling at thirty miles an hour and a stone is thrown in front of it at thirty miles an hour what is the speed of the stone when it hits the hiker? Answer, sixty miles an hour. Pretty straightforward. But let's forget the stone and instead imagine the man in the car flashing his headlights to tell the hiker to get the hell out of the way. Does the light from the headlights travel towards the hiker at 186,282 point . . .

PROFESSOR: 397 . . .

ACTRESS: Miles per second plus 30 miles per hour? Answer, no! Because the speed of light is always the same. Did you ever prove that hypothesis?

PROFESSOR: It was never disproved.

ACTRESS: Let's hope it never is.

PROFESSOR: Amen.

ACTRESS: So where light is concerned you have to think tricky because you can throw your flashlight as hard as you like at the hiker, but the light itself won't hit him any sooner.

She has by this time dropped, thrown or

manoeuvred a book, a small flashlight, a
magazine with an automobile on the front
and a little toy model of Charlie Chaplin.
Now she reveals her pièce de résistance,
two little trains with track.

Now. Here we go. We have to imagine
two locomotives speeding past each other
at a hell of a speed. A red one and a green
one. The driver of each locomotive has a
flashlight which he turns on at the precise
moment they pass each other. Now the
light from the flashlight travels at the
same speed regardless of the speeds of the
flashlights themselves so both flashes
expand in all directions just like a single
sphere of light. Now the driver of the red
locomotive watches the light spread out at
the same speed in all directions at once
and regardless of the fact he's moving
very fast thataway . . . (*She points left.*)
. . . he stays with the centre of the sphere
of light that came from his flashlight, both
flashlights. And if he looks over at the
green locomotive he'll see that the driver
of the green train has moved thataway . . .
(*She points right.*) . . . and is therefore not
at the centre of light anymore. I know,
you're way ahead of me. Everything's just
fine until you look at it from the point of
view of the driver of the green train. He
too remember flashed his light and he too
watches it spread out at the same speed in
all directions at once regardless, and so he
too stays with the centre of the sphere of
light and looks over to see the red
locomotive has moved like crazy
thataway! . . .

She points left.

. . . And isn't in the centre of the light
anymore. So both drivers think they're
the ones in the centre of the light while
the other driver has moved on past.
Question, which one is right. Answer,
both of them! Not only that. I figured out
what would happen if you just stood on
the tracks and watched. The light would
stay with you and the trains would both
vamoose and you'd be right too!

PROFESSOR: That's remarkably . . .

ACTRESS: That's not all. If we stand on
the tracks a little longer you know what
happens?

PROFESSOR: We get run over?

Silence.

I stay behind afterwards and clean the
board.

ACTRESS: I don't like to be patronised.

PROFESSOR: I'm sorry.

ACTRESS: I accept your apology.
Anyway, if we watch from the tracks a
little longer we see that the distance
between the light and the green train after
a few seconds is the same as the distance
between the light and the red train, but
the driver of the green train thinks his
distance from it is much less than the red
train's distance, I mean no distance at all,
and vice-versa, the driver of the red train
thinks his distance from the light is less.
You know what that means?

PROFESSOR: Yes.

ACTRESS: It means that distances
measured are always shorter if you
measure them yourself rather than get
someone else to do it. And it's not just
distances, it's time as well. Have you got a
watch, can we use it? We have to imagine
this room is the universe. We begin
together somewhere in space time at
exactly five o'clock and we synchronise.

PROFESSOR: Five o'clock.

ACTRESS: Five o'clock. Now I travel away
from you at a heck of a speed, let's say one
fifth of the speed of light, and I travel for
five minutes and it gets me here. Now my
watch says five past five but it isn't very
reliable so I look across to check what
your watch says and what does it say?

PROFESSOR: Five past five.

ACTRESS: Not to me it don't. It says four
minutes past five because five minutes
past five hasn't reached yet. I don't see
a minute ticked off on your watch until a
minute later than you because it takes a
minute for me to see your watch because
light is taking another minute to get here,
see? So now I travel away for another five
minutes, put your watch on five minutes,
until my watch says ten past five and I
look across and your watch says, wait for
it, eight minutes past five which means
that your watch is getting slower and
slower!! Now here comes the really
exciting part. I say your watch says eight
minutes past five, what do you say your
watch says?

PROFESSOR: Ten minutes past five.

ACTRESS: But that's what I say mine says. Now here's the thousand dollar question. Remember that if you look at my watch it's going to take the light two minutes to reach you. What do you say my watch says?

PROFESSOR: Eight minutes past five?

Pause.

ACTRESS: Which means that I say you're going more slowly than me while you say I'm going more slowly than you.

PROFESSOR: Beautiful.

ACTRESS: So, the main point I have demonstrated is that all measurements of time and space are necessarily made relative to the observer, and are not necessarily the same for two independent observers. That is the Specific Theory of Relativity! Isn't it?

Pause.

PROFESSOR: Yes it is.

She sighs a huge sigh of relief and falls back on the bed.

ACTRESS: Now you have to show me your legs.

PROFESSOR (*rolls his trousers up around his knees*): I promise never to display these in public if you promise never to lecture in Nuclear Physics.

ACTRESS: Done.

PROFESSOR: How far did you get with the General Theory?

ACTRESS: Oh, I know that too. All the way through. Only I didn't understand a word of it.

PROFESSOR: You learned it without understanding it?

ACTRESS: Mmmhmm. It's like riding on the subway. I know where I get on and where to get off but while I'm travelling I don't know where the hell I am. I suppose you must, but then you dug all the tunnels. Still, I know the premise and the results, that's the main thing.

PROFESSOR: That's nothing. Knowledge is nothing without understanding. Let me tell you this. This watch we used. My father gave it to me when I was five years old, anything precious he used to give away. It regulated the world and helped me understand one day at a time. Sunrise at five, sunset at nine, dinner at twelve and father home at seven. Then one week I was ill in bed, my watch by my side, observing the world through the little window, and my father brought me another small gift. It was a little stump of metal about so long. I asked what it was. Was it precious, what should I do with it, what did it do? My father told me to find out. Three days I didn't learn what it was; the world stayed the same; a known quantity, but then on the third day I reached from the bedside table and it jumps! It catches the little piece of metal and it carries it up. It is a little magnet and it pulled my world apart. So I studied, and now I understand magnetism. I know the truth of magnetism. This is why you must not pretend to have grasped the General Theory. You may know a great deal but without understanding you will never know the truth.

ACTRESS: You mean it's no use knowing how many beans make ten if you haven't learned to count to five.

PROFESSOR: Probably, yes.

ACTRESS: Well, I don't know if that's what you mean but that's how I understand it.

PROFESSOR: You're too bright for your own good. You know too much and understand too little.

ACTRESS: I understand that I was born and that I'm still living.

PROFESSOR: So?

ACTRESS: So don't talk to me as if I were a child.

PROFESSOR: Liebchen . . .

ACTRESS: There was a woman reporter once who asked me in the middle of an interview for *Harpers* how long a whale could stay underwater before it drowned. (*Pause.*) She said it was a kind of intelligence test.

PROFESSOR: Whose intelligence was at stake, hers or yours?

ACTRESS: It doesn't matter. What matters is I didn't know and I thought it mattered. So I try to know things, is that so wrong.

PROFESSOR: If I told you the moon is made of cheese would you believe me?

ACTRESS: No.

PROFESSOR: If I told you it was made of granite?

ACTRESS: Maybe.

PROFESSOR: If I told you I knew for certain?

ACTRESS: I'd believe you.

PROFESSOR: So now you know the moon is made of granite.

ACTRESS: Yes.

PROFESSOR: But it isn't.

ACTRESS: I only said I knew because you said you knew.

PROFESSOR: Precisely, but I was wrong. Knowledge is not truth, it is merely agreement. You agree with me, we agree with someone else, we all have knowledge but we get no closer to the truth of the moon. You cannot understand by making definitions, only by turning over the possibilities. It's called thinking. I know, something I know, is that there are men, there are such men; I know of greed, I know of hate, I know of evil, but I do not, I will not, understand these things. If I say I know, I stop thinking, but so long as I think, I come to understand, I might approach some truth.

ACTRESS: This is the best conversation I ever had.

He puts away his watch, sits wearily.

Is it over?

PROFESSOR: I think it had better be.

She rises. He finds her coat. She doesn't put it on.

ACTRESS: A girlfriend and I played a game a few years back. We each made a list of the men it would be nicest to sleep with. You came third on mine.

PROFESSOR: Third?

ACTRESS: Then we worked out how old you are.

PROFESSOR: And you struck me off.

ACTRESS: No, I moved you to the top.

Pause.

PROFESSOR: No. Thank you for considering me.

ACTRESS: You can't just throw me on the streets at this hour.

PROFESSOR: You are absolutely right. You are welcome to stay. I shall sleep in the bathtub.

ACTRESS: That would be absurdly uncomfortable.

PROFESSOR: A fine American tradition.

ACTRESS: A man of your age.

PROFESSOR: Precisely.

He takes some bedding from the bed.

ACTRESS: You can't sleep in the bath.

PROFESSOR: What's good enough for Cary Grant is good enough for me.

ACTRESS: Wouldn't it be nice to share the bed. We don't have to make love. Personally I think you'd be a damn fool not to.

Pause.

PROFESSOR: I think I have to be a damn fool. (*She puts on her coat.*) Perhap I could give you my telephone number. You'd be very welcome to visit me at my home.

ACTRESS: Nonsense. I might end up on first name terms with your telephone service but you'd never find time for me.

PROFESSOR: I have no service. I have a secretary, whose first name is still a mystery after four years. I have a small house on a large river full of fish which I can't catch and I have a great deal of time to offer.

ACTRESS: I'm sorry. I have none to give you, beyond now. The little time my work leaves me, my husband demands, what he leaves I need for myself, and Dostoievsky steals most of that. I hoped we could just . . . come together, you know, in the middle of all this, for an hour or so.

PROFESSOR: Then don't go. (*She smiles.*) But I sleep in the bathtub. If two people do not give each other time, they give each other nothing.

She goes to the window and looks out at the flashing neon. He has embarrassed her. He takes the bedding into the bathroom.

ACTRESS: Time is relative too,

remember. If we were born at exactly the same time, were exactly the same age, and yet I was to travel away from you and back again at some fantastic speed to some corner of the galaxy, when I got back I'd be younger than you. Wouldn't I?

PROFESSOR: Yes you would.

ACTRESS: And you proved that. I really would be younger, which means the less you move the faster you grow old. It means you've got to keep moving.

PROFESSOR: I suppose it does.

ACTRESS: So then why won't you sleep with me?

PROFESSOR: Because I could never end up younger.

She moves to the pile of calculus, kneels beside it and embraces it.

ACTRESS: You're calculating the shape of space, right?

PROFESSOR: Absolutely.

ACTRESS: When you've finished this you will have expressed the precise nature of the physical universe, right?

PROFESSOR: So?

She leaves the calculus and touches his leg.

ACTRESS: So do it tomorrow. It'll be here. I won't.

She goes to the window.

I wish they'd switch me off.

PROFESSOR: I prefer to look up.

ACTRESS: Stars are too far away. They make me feel small and lonely. Sad.

PROFESSOR: Me too, small and lonely, but not sad. All who look, feel as small and lonely as the rest. Doesn't that make you feel happier?

ACTRESS: A little.

PROFESSOR: Smallness happens and aloneness happens but the miracle is that insignificance doesn't happen. The stars tell us we can walk on the grass, talk to anyone we meet, touch those people, ask anything of them; the stars won't think the worse of you. The stars won't even notice.

Pause.

So, what the hell.

He fetches the bedding back from the bathroom.
He sits on the bed clutching his pillow.
She starts to undress.
He winds his alarm clock.

PROFESSOR: Is it late or early?

ACTRESS: It's relative. Your watch is just there.

PROFESSOR: It hasn't told me the time since I was seven years old.

ACTRESS: Did you drop it?

PROFESSOR: No, I picked it up, with a large electro-magnet.

She shows him her watch. They continue undressing.
There is a loud knocking on the door.

BALLPLAYER (*off*): Open the door you dumb broad, I know you're in there.

Pause.

You in there?

Three loud bangs.

ACTRESS: You are, I'm not.

PROFESSOR (*whispers*): Who is it?

ACTRESS: Just a fan.

PROFESSOR: Do all your fans pursue you so persistently?

ACTRESS: Only those I marry.

BALLPLAYER (*off*): You want me to go get a pass key? I only have to sign my name and the nightman'd open this door damn fast, you know that.

PROFESSOR: He is famous?

ACTRESS: He hit home safely in fifty-six consecutive games with an average of a hundred and thirty-five. He's God. He can open most doors . . .

Heavy thump.

One way or the other.

PROFESSOR: Shall I let him in?

ACTRESS: No, he's angry.

PROFESSOR: You think if we keep the door closed he'll get happy?

BALLPLAYER: You hiding yourself in the john? I'm going to look in the john . . .

There's no place to hide; I'm gonna kill you.

PROFESSOR: Would he harm you with me here?

ACTRESSS (*with a glance at the window*): No, he'd harm me with you face down on the sidewalk.

Three thumps on the door.

I think he's just angry, not livid, the way he's banging.

PROFESSOR: How can you tell?

Thump.

ACTRESS: He's not using his head.

PROFESSOR: I go and talk to him.

ACTRESS: Wait until I've figured what mood he's in . . .

Another thump disuades the PROFESSOR *from opening the door.*

PROFESSOR: Ya, was ist das denn, was kann ich für ihn machen?

Pause.

BALLPLAYER: So you finally slept with the delicatessen. You speak English?

PROFESSOR: Ich kann nicht lügen. Yes, I do.

BALLPLAYER: So is my wife in there with you?

PROFESSOR: Do you think she would like to be found in another man's room? Would it be a good thing to find her?

BALLPLAYER: You a man of honour?

PROFESSOR: I hope so.

BALLPLAYER: You'd tell me straight if she was there?

PROFESSOR: If you ask me straight, I will tell you, yes.

Pause.

BALLPLAYER: I'll tell you what I'm going to do. I'm going to count to ten. If she's in there then you open the door and let me get at her, OK? If she's not there you tell me so and as a man of honour I'll believe you and leave you to sleep. OK, I'm going to count to ten.

ACTRESS: You never counted past three in your life, you dumb ox!

BALLPLAYER (*off*): Shit.

ACTRESS: One, two, three, home; that's as far as you ever bothered to go.

Silence.

PROFESSOR: You think he's gone?

Biggest thump yet as the BALLPLAYER *throws himself at the door.*

ACTRESS: Uh uh. But he's in quite good control: you almost has a conversation. I'm going to let him in. Lock yourself in the bathroom.

PROFESSOR: Certainly not.

ACTRESS: OK. If he goes like that . . . (*She hits her head with her fist.*) . . . make straight for the elevator. If he cracks his knuckles, let him speak.

The BALLPLAYER *is throwing himself at the door regularly. The* ACTRESS *carefully sets herself up to open it for him to fly into the room. She opens it wide. He is nowhere to be seen. He then steps casually into the doorway.*

BALLPLAYER: You think I'm dumb or some . . .

She throws the door in his face.

ACTRESS: Yes, I think you're dumb.

BALLPLAYER: You crazy? You made my nose bleed.

PROFESSOR: I'll get a damp cloth.

He goes into the bathroom. The ACTRESS *sits the* BALLPLAYER *down.*

BALLPLAYER: Why'd you pull a stunt like that?

ACTRESS: What happens when you're angry?

BALLPLAYER: I hit out.

ACTRESSS: And what happens when you see blood?

BALLPLAYER: You know I go limp, I can't help it.

ACTRESS: That's all right honey, I prefer you this way.

BALLPLAYER: I'm still angry.

ACTRESS: I know, but listen to this. If you so much as make a move towards that old man, then be warned, I'll take off through the door and that's the last you'll see of me for a long time.

BALLPLAYER: That's a very big joke. I want to see my wife I just go to the movies. I want to see my wife's underwear I just walk down to the corner like all the other guys.

The PROFESSOR *returns with a face cloth.*

PROFESSOR: Would you like this where . . .?

The BALLPLAYER *snatches it.*

BALLPLAYER: My nose never bled before. I got cracked on the nose once by a high ball and the pitcher's nose bled.

PROFESSOR: Down your back I think it's meant to go.

BALLPLAYER: So you got screwed by another shrink?

ACTRESS: He's not a shrink, he's a friend, and we were talking.

BALLPLAYER: Talking at five in the morning?

PROFESSOR: It's hard to believe, perhaps.

BALLPLAYER: No, it's not hard to believe. If she can talk through the entire World Series she can talk until five any morning. She talk smart to you?

PROFESSOR: Yes she did.

BALLPLAYER: You should have cracked your knuckles a couple of times; that's the only thing stops her. Why you got no clothes on?

The PROFESSOR *has no shoes or shirt.*

PROFESSOR: It's a dog of a night.

BALLPLAYER: Ain't it. What sort of therapy do you do?

PROFESSOR: I'm a physicist.

BALLPLAYER: He mean massage?

ACTRESS: OK, you were right the first time; he's a shrink.

BALLPLAYER: Get your coat.

ACTRESS: I'll follow you when I've finished my talking.

BALLPLAYER: I said get your coat!

Pause.

BALLPLAYER: OK, finish. Tell her what Floyd would have said.

PROFESSOR: Floyd?

ACTRESS: Freud.

BALLPLAYER: She's been to a dozen shrinks. She tells you how she hated her mother and so can't have stable relationships then you tell her the reason she can't have stable relationships is because she hated her mother and she pays you fifty dollars and she comes back next week until you make a pass and she goes and finds another shrink. I seen it all before, me and Floyd, we're old buddies.

ACTRESS: Fer-oid!

BALLPLAYER: One shrink told her she had a father fixation for this man Floyd. You guys are driving her nuts.

PROFESSOR: I'm not a therapist.

BALLPLAYER: I've met her mother, and let me tell you, she's easy to hate. Anyone who hates her mother, there's nothing wrong with them.

ACTRESS: Stepmother.

BALLPLAYER: I hate you guys, bunch of . . .

ACTRESS: Will you sit down and shut up!

He shuts up, but will not sit.

The Professor is not a psychiatrist, he's an old friend of mine.

BALLPLAYER: Intellectual?

ACTRESS: We have never even touched.–

BALLPLAYER: She has two types of friend.

ACTRESS: The type he doesn't understand and the type he assaults.

BALLPLAYER: I think you're a man of honour; I've got a nose for that sort of thing. Go ahead, talk smart. (*He sits and opens a pack of gum, looks at the card, discards it.*)

ACTRESS: Where were we?

PROFESSOR: Mmm?

BALLPLAYER: You were discussing her head.

ACTRESS: As it happens we were

discussing the shape of the physical universe.

BALLPLAYER: Easy ones first, huh.

ACTRESS: If you'd like to contribute I suppose we could discuss something we all know about but that would limit us to the last World Series and the names of the seven dwarves.

BALLPLAYER: Shift!

ACTRESS: Go screw!

BALLPLAYER: One . . .

ACTRESS: The shape of the universe.

BALLPLAYER: . . . two . . .

PROFESSOR: I think this is not the best time.

BALLPLAYER: . . . . three . . .

ACTRESS: Please, he's still angry. Try four.

BALLPLAYER: Home! The man don't want to talk. He don't have nothing to say, so get off your butt and come home.

ACTRESS: Truman or Eisenhower?

Pause. BALLPLAYER *sits.*

Please, the shape of the universe or something.

PROFESSOR: It's not important; you have things to discuss.

ACTRESS: We had a discussion last month, about the presidential candidates and their policies. To underline his points about *détente*, Honey here hit me with a baseball bat

BALLPLAYER: You embarrassed the man now.

ACTRESS: . . . It'd be nice if we could talk while he sat in a corner and remembered how easily I bruise when he's around.

BALLPLAYER: She's right; I hit out; we discussed it though, it ain't purposeful. (*He moves away.*) So go ahead, talk smart.

ACTRESS: Please.

PROFESSOR: Well. The shape of the universe has to be considered in four dimensional terms with time as the fourth dimension.

He is distracted by the BALLPLAYER

swinging an imaginary baseball bat.

Therefore the shape of the universe is impossible to visualise, but it can just be imagined.

ACTRESS: We have to use our imaginations, honey. Can you imagine that?

PROFESSOR: Er — space has no boundaries but neither is it infinite. That is our starting point.

The BALLPLAYER *opens another pack of gum, looks at the card, discards it.*

Consider one dimension first. Consider length without breadth or width. As a model, a very thin length of rope.

ACTRESS: Or a shoelace?

PROFESSOR: A shoelace if you like.

She unties one of the BALLPLAYER's *shoelaces.*

BALLPLAYER: Hey, that's a Pipers Brogue shoelace, you can only get those with the shoes.

ACTRESS: Don't be a baby, this is science.

BALLPLAYER: She thinks I'm stupid, but it's just I watch TV a lot, you know?

ACTRESS: Length. No breadth or width, hardly.

PROFESSOR: Thank you. Now considered in one dimensional terms this shoelace is obviously not infinite in length, but it does have boundaries; it has two ends. To make it resemble space it must have no boundaries, so what must we do with the shoelace?

The BALLPLAYER *snatches the lace.*

BALLPLAYER: How about using it to tie up your shoe?

PROFESSOR: Very close. You must tie a knot, get rid of the ends.

The ACTRESS *snatches the shoelace back and ties a knot, tugging it tight.*

ACTRESS: A shoelace without infinite length or boundaries. A circle.

PROFESSOR: Bravo. But remember, a one-dimensional circle. It is really a rather unusual straight line.

BALLPLAYER: It's a useless fucking shoelace, I know that.

PROFESSOR: Now let us think one step further, in two dimensions. Let us think of something that has length and breadth but no width. What would be a suitable model?

ACTRESS: A sheet of paper.

The BALLPLAYER *pops gum. She glares at him.*

BALLPLAYER: Sorry. She hates that sound. We made a pact; I don't pop gum and she don't pop nembutal.

She takes part of her shooting script from her bag or coat and tears out a page. The BALLPLAYER *sits between them and watches like a player on the bench.*

ACTRESS: Length and breadth. No width.

PROFESSOR: Now is it infinite?

ACTRESS: No, it's finite, but it has boundaries all round the edge.

PROFESSOR: So how do we make it without boundaries?

ACTRESS: Stretch it out? Keep stretching?

PROFESSOR: No, that would make it infinite.

BALLPLAYER (*pops gum*): I did it without thinking.

ACTRESS: Is there anything you do any other way?

BALLPLAYER: Pardon me for breathing.

ACTRESS: That's the only thing. Your entire life is a reflex action. Your final breath won't be a rattle, it'll be a pop.

PROFESSOR: The question is how can an object existing on two planes be finite but have no boundaries?

ACTRESS: I give up.

PROFESSOR: You work it out, then we go on.

She thinks. The BALLPLAYER *blows a bubble.*

ACTRESS: Don't you dare. (*She holds out her hand. He gives her the bubble.*) A bubble, curl it up and make it into a bubble, a ball, a sphere.

PROFESSOR: Yes, but a sphere in two dimensions, not three.

ACTRESS: How can a ball come in two dimensions?

BALLPLAYER: Baseballs come in two dimensions. A league ball's three eighths of an inch bigger than a World series ball. Like a baseball, right?

ACTRESS: You dumb ox.

BALLPLAYER: Don't you call me no ox. That's a joke, PeeWee says that. You watch Bilko?

ACTRESS: Like a baseball.

PROFESSOR: Like the surface of a baseball, as if it had no centre, only the leather surround.

BALLPLAYER: A hollow baseball.

PROFESSOR: Exactly.

BALLPLAYER: See, the shape of the universe is like a baseball, only bigger, natch. Like we're in a baseball.

PROFESSOR: Not exactly in, no. On.

BALLPLAYER: Oh, right. Gravitational pull.

ACTRESS: I got it. Like we can think of this planet in two dimensions; north-south and east-west, then it's surface has no boundaries but it isn't infinite.

PROFESSOR: Right. Now the next and final step is impossible to visualise. We are in three dimensions and we have to start with a real sphere, a solid baseball. It is finite of course, but it does have boundaries. Imagine a baseball without boundaries and you are in the fourth dimension.

BALLPLAYER: You got a baseball without boundaries and you got no chance of a home run, I know that.

PROFESSOR: From a line to a circle, from a circle to a sphere, from a sphere to . . . the shape of the Universe.

ACTRESS: Wow. What? Say it again. Say it again.

PROFESSOR: It has to do with motion. The line was given motion. The line was given motion through the second dimension, the circle was given motion through the third, and the sphere is given motion through the fourth, through time. The universe is in constant motion through time. You can come closest if you try to imagine turning something absolutely solid inside out, and keep turning it inside out forever.

ACTRESS: Wow.

BALLPLAYER: Bullshit. I've told you what I think. I think it's round, like everything else in nature, the sun, moon, flowers, are all based on a circle, you noticed that? Like the world. I don't know what shape you two geniuses think the old world is but me and Columbus think it's round which is a damn lucky thing for the States because if it wasn't for Columbus we'd all be Indians, you ever think of that? Get your coat.

ACTRESS: I'm not coming.

BALLPLAYER: Why not?

ACTRESS: Because you're an idiot. Answer me one question.

JIM: What?

ACTRESS: How long can a whale stay underwater before it drowns?

BALLPLAYER: How the fuck should I know?

ACTRESS: Guess.

BALLPLAYER: You expect me to say forever, but I ain't that stupid, a whale ain't no fish. It breathes like you talk, out the top of its head. Two, three minutes, right?

ACTRESS: Uh huh?

PROFESSOR: Is he right?

ACTRESS: How the fuck should I know?

BALLPLAYER: Here! (*He throws her her coat.*)

ACTRESS: I'm not coming.

BALLPLAYER: I ain't angry.

ACTRESS: I'm tired.

BALLPLAYER: I have to talk to you.

ACTRESS: There's nothing to talk about.

BALLPLAYER: You spend all night whoring around in front of a coupla hundred bozos and that's nothing to talk about?

ACTRESS: You see this, it's a smile. It doesn't mean I'm happy, it means I'm smiling. That's what actresses do and that's what I am.

BALLPLAYER: You enjoy men looking up your legs for three hours?

ACTRESS: I hate it.

BALLPLAYER: Then quit.

ACTRESS: The only thing I hate more than a man looking at my legs is a man expecting me to wear them out cooking him TV dinners.

The PROFESSOR *retires to the bathroom. The* BALLPLAYER *pops gum.*

You remember my first orgasm?

BALLPLAYER: Yep.

ACTRESS: Afterwards I lay in the dark, utterly exhausted, hoping you might light me a cigarette and what did I hear? Pop. That's all I ever hear now; pathetic little explosions, that's all I get from you.

BALLPLAYER: You want a divorce?

The PROFESSOR *returns, takes his pad and goes back to the bathroom.*

You want to finish it?

ACTRESS: No.

BALLPLAYER: Then come home. You come home, honey, or I swear I'll go get me a lawyer and I'll disappear so's you can't find me for a change. Bob Dalrymple, he gave me the name of a good man. Look, I wrote it down. I phoned this man. He said with the reputation you got I'd have no trouble at all. He said it'd be a pleasure.

ACTRESS: You phoned a lawyer?

BALLPLAYER: You ain't been home for three weeks.

ACTRESS: OK.

BALLPLAYER: You coming home?

ACTRESS: Mmmhmm.

BALLPLAYER: OK.

The PROFESSOR *enters again.*

PROFESSOR: Excuse me, I have to get this . . .

BALLPLAYER: It's OK, we're leaving now.

ACTRESS: I have to use the bathroom first.

She goes.

BALLPLAYER: Baby, leave the door.

She leaves the door ajar. The men sit on the bed, side by side.

You chew gum?

PROFESSOR: No. (*He takes a piece.*) Thank you.

BALLPLAYER (*takes out the card*): Huh. Who the hell's Willy McKormak? You ever heard of Willy McKormak?

PROFESSOR: No.

BALLPLAYER: Some punk kid thinks he's a bigshot, they put him on a bubble gum card. (*He throws it away.*) You know how many bubble gum series I been in? Thirteen. Thirteen series. I been in Chigley's Sporting Greats, I been in Pinky's World Series Stars 1936, 1937, 1939, 1942, 1944, 1945, 1949 and 1951. I been in Tip Top Boy's Best Baseball Tips showing how best to pitch, swing, deadstop and slide, and I have been Hubbly Bubbly's Baseball Bites best all-rounder nine years running. So no, hey! Hold on. That's 13 series but . . . 21 separate editions all told. And how many kids you know collect? Card for card it must run into millions. I must be stuck in albums from here to the Pacific. World wide. They give gum to little Chink kids, don't they? You liberate them one day, next day they're making swops. I saw on TV they don't take beads and stuff up the Amazon no more; they take instant coffee and bubble gum. I could go into a little village in Africa that's hardly seen a whiteman and they'd say 'Hi Big Hitter, sit down and have some coffee.' This fame thing's enough to give you the heebies, I can tell you. Chigleys, Pinkys, Hubblys and Tip Top. That's some bubble gum.

PROFESSOR: I was on Lucky Strike Great Scientific Achievements.

Pause.

It's not much though, compared with . . .

BALLPLAYER: Thirteen series.

PROFESSOR: Thirteen series.

BALLPLAYER: 21 separate cards. You got a claim though, somebody must have heard of you. You just hope they never start recognising you on the streets, that's hell, I can tell you. But I ain't complaining, no sir. I ain't bought a drink since 1943. You OK honey?

ACTRESS (*from bathroom*): I'm OK.

BALLPLAYER: You like my wife?

PROFESSOR: She's very intelligent.

BALLPLAYER: You don't think she's beautiful?

PROFESSOR: Also.

BALLPLAYER: You ask her here?

PROFESSOR: I think she was feeling lonely with all those people.

BALLPLAYER: Then she should have come home. I like you, I don't believe there could have been any funny business, but let me tell you something; she's smart enough with all that science talk but it don't mean nothing compared to feelings, you know that? I could kill a man, you know? If she ever got it down to one. You know, I get so tightened up, like just before a game, whenever I'm not alone with her. I get so mad because everytime I'm up there hitting she's stealing away every chance she gets and because even the team, my old team, they'd rather stare at her than gab about old times. They treat her like a star or something. I'll tell you, never put a woman up on a pedestal, it's too easy for her to kick your teeth down your throat. You know what she needs? She needs a thousand people touching her all of the time and she needs to be alone all of the time also. She's crazy, except when she's with me, then she's whole, you know, peaceful. Except she don't see it. I get so tightened up, like I used to waiting to run into the stadium, except now it's all tunnel, there's no . . .

He tries to indicate the stadium, the sun, the crowds.

So I hit out.

He takes up his imaginary bat.

Sometimes she got in the way, so I stopped using a bat. (*He takes a swing.*) Nyah!

ACTRESS: Honey, steady.

BALLPLAYER: Baby?

ACTRESS: I'm OK.

BALLPLAYER: You bleeding again?

ACTRESS: Will you please leave me alone so I can pull myself together.

BALLPLAYER: If I did you think she could?

There is a chink of glass on enamel from the bathroom, then a loud crash. The men leap up.

Baby!

ACTRESS (*enters*): OK. I'm OK.

She passes out. The BALLPLAYER picks her up.

PROFESSOR: Put her to bed. I shall get a doctor.

BALLPLAYER: No, she does this all the time. You fetch a doctor and she'll give you hell.

PROFESSOR: But she might be ill.

BALLPLAYER: Yeh, she's ill, but she's OK. She always faints in strange bathrooms; she's anaemic. She bleeds, you know? She's loose inside. She can't keep a baby in after it gets so big. They keep trying to tighten her up, she keeps getting loose again. A baby could kill her 'cos to keep it they'd have made her so tight it couldn't come out natural, you know? Something like that. So she feels really bad most of the time.

PROFESSOR: I think we ought to get a doctor.

BALLPLAYER: She always has one she trusts, until he fucks her over and she has to find another. (*He finds a card in her coat.*) Call him direct, from the lobby.

PROFESSOR: Keep her warm, or whatever you do.

*The PROFESSOR leaves.
The BALLPLAYER takes up an imaginary bat and ball which he tosses high once or twice. He hits the ball with all his might.*

BALLPLAYER: Nyaah!! Let me tell you, you, you may be all bright lights on the outside but on the inside you fell down from up there and hit the sidewalk. Inside you're damaged, you're broken and bruised, until I don't want to love you anymore. How can I make love to a wound? Nothing heals if you fuck around. If there's something wrong with you it's no good peck, peck, pecking at it; you'll just end up all feather and bone.

He looks at the neon.

You think that's you, you fucking mess, you think that's you?

*With his imaginary bat he suddenly smashes into her; repeatedly hits her pelvis, her breasts, her head.
She comes to.*

ACTRESS: Honey?

BALLPLAYER (*gently*): You did it again.

ACTRESS: I'm OK.

BALLPLAYER: You're a mess.

ACTRESS: I could never be a suicide! I tried to take an aspirin, took one look at the bottle and hit the floor.

BALLPLAYER: I have to say sorry.

ACTRESS: Why?

BALLPLAYER: I hit you with the bat again, while you were out.

ACTRESS: I prefer it that way.

BALLPLAYER: I really piss you off, don't I?

ACTRESS: You're my mirror. I see all the little things you do as in a mirror.

BALLPLAYER: You see you in me?

ACTRESS: No, I see you.

BALLPLAYER: Not a hell of a lot you don't. You mean you and me are a lot alike?

He finds tablets in her coat and gives her two.

ACTRESS: We're not at all alike. It's just that things you do strike chords in me that resonate so deeply I don't want to lose you for fear of never hearing them again.

BALLPLAYER: We sound the same?

ACTRESS: All I wish is you weren't so stupid.

BALLPLAYER: I remind you of the sidewalk, I'm a mirror, I sound like you sound like. You spend half your life talking bull and I'm stupid.

ACTRESS: I'm trying to communicate with you without resorting to batting averages. I'm trying to tell you how I love you.

BALLPLAYER: Not a hell of a lot.

ACTRESS: Not how much or how well, how.

BALLPLAYER: How?

ACTRESS: In my way.

BALLPLAYER: What about my way?

ACTRESS: What's that?

BALLPLAYER: My way? What I want.

Enter the PROFESSOR. *The* BALLPLAYER *unwraps more gum.*

PROFESSOR: Doctor Steinberg is fishing in New Jersey.

ACTRESS: I'm fine really.

He gathers some of his things.

PROFESSOR: I had a small word with the night porter. He's going to find me a room on another floor. No, stay, please, you sleep, get well. And please, be my guest.

BALLPLAYER (*finds himself on a card*): Hey! See what I mean, every five or six packs. Here, impress your grandchildren.

PROFESSOR (*accepts*): Thank you. Toothbrush. (*He goes into the bathroom.*)

The dawn chorus begins.
The BALLPLAYER *blows a bubble, stops himself just in time.*

ACTRESS: Do you still want a child?

He very carefully sucks his bubble back into his mouth.

BALLPLAYER: I want the one we already had.

ACTRESS: I was under contract. I'll be careful.

BALLPLAYER: I don't care no more. (*He clambers onto the bed and eventually curls up, his head in her lap, having stuck his gum behind his ear.*)

ACTRESS: It might be a son.

BALLPLAYER: And it might be a fucking mess.

ACTRESS: I'm highly strung, not a hereditary disease. I want to be pregnant.

BALLPLAYER: It'd never get born.

ACTRESS: This one will.

BALLPLAYER: It'd tear you up. What they don't tear up, you tear up yourself.

ACTRESS: Not all my life. Something's got to give. I want . . . If it happens . . . a daughter. A son?

He is asleep.

Honey? I think I am.

The PROFESSOR *crosses with his spongebag. They look at each other. She gestures, clutching faintly for something she doubts she'll ever attain. Her hand goes to her face and she begins to weep.*
The PROFESSOR *picks up his calculus, clutches it to him, and leaves.*

Act Two
The ACTRESS *is alone, asleep. She is in
bed. Her dress lies on a chair.*
There is a quiet knock on the door.

SENATOR: Professor?

He opens the door. The ACTRESS *is
asleep, her back to him.*

I brought you up a little breakfast. It's
eight o'clock. Professor?

*She wakes and turns looking and feeling
quite a mess. She focuses on the*
SENATOR *who gapes momentarily.*

I do apologise, I must have gotten out at
the wrong floor. All these rooms do look
the same.

*She puts on her dark glasses. He notices
the blackboard and checks the room
number.*

This is room six-fourteen; Professor's
room.

ACTRESS: He moved. I don't know
where.

SENATOR: Has anyone ever told you, you
could be the splitting image . . .

ACTRESS: I know, if I was six years
younger and took more care.

SENATOR: Right. (*She takes pills.*) Will he
be coming back? Only I had arranged to
meet him.

ACTRESS: Perhaps you'll find him in the
lobby.

SENATOR: Would you mind if I used the
washroom?

ACTRESS: He's not in there. I told you he
took another room.

SENATOR: Well I can tell you that
wherever he is he's certainly shot up in my
estimation. Do you mind if I wait?

ACTRESS: Not if you don't mind my
throwing up.

SENATOR: Shame to let the coffee go
cold. Please, help yourself. You've taken
a dislike to me, I can tell. It's my fault,
I've been insensitive. Please accept this
little solatium from me to you. A solatium
is a small gift in recompense for
inconvenience or wounded feelings. (*He
puts the tray beside the bed.*) You know,
you could be sisters. Must be kind of
advantageous for a girl like you.

ACTRESS: Are you a friend of the
Professor's?

SENATOR: We're just good friends. You
could say that he and I are both seekers
after knowledge in our own ways. We
pick up little things and turn them over in
our minds. Word for today is solipsism;
you want to know what solipsism means?

ACTRESS: It's the belief that only you
exist, that everything else exists in your
imagination.

SENATOR: College girl too, huh? Well,
notice you said *you* meaning me rather
than *me* meaning you. You explained that
only *I* exist, not that only *you* exist. That
kind of gives the theory weight from my
point of view.

ACTRESS: Lucky for you I'm not a
solipsist.

SENATOR: Why's that?

ACTRESS: I can't imagine inventing you.

SENATOR: Would you pass me the toast?

ACTRESS: Imagine some.

SENATOR: I did. There it is.

ACTRESS: Imagine it closer why don't
you.

SENATOR: Because that's why I invented
you.

A knock on the door.

ACTRESS: Come in.

The PROFESSOR *enters.*

SENATOR: Good morning Professor, I
brought you up some breakfast. I been
having a little chat with your college
friend here about solipsism. I'm deeply
committed to the concept; I should be,
after all I invented it.

PROFESSOR: Have you been disturbed?

ACTRESS: Profoundly.

PROFESSOR: Would you leave now
please.

SENATOR: Can't be done, Professor. We
got business first. I was going to remind
you of the mud soliflucting your way but it
seems like you're involved in a major
landslide right here. I mean I could have
been the bellboy; you'd have had a fleet
of photographers hanging on your door

right now. Lucky for you I'm a man of the world.

ACTRESS: Who is this?

PROFESSOR: A representative of the people. I am supposed to appear before the UnAmerican Committee today. The senator wishes to compose my testimony for me.

ACTRESS: Then tell him to go screw.

PROFESSOR: Go screw.

ACTRESS: Goes for me too.

SENATOR: Are you willing to testify?

PROFESSOR: No.

SENATOR: Then I have to warn you, you may be subject to an investigation into your political activities. I have reason to suspect you of conspiracy to overthrow the US government.

ACTRESS: He's got to be kidding.

SENATOR: Sounds good though, don't it? That's how it goes in the book. This is all by the book. The book is what the people pay me for.

ACTRESS: Is he for real?

SENATOR: You think I'm not?

ACTRESS: I think you're fat.

SENATOR: You're very charming.

ACTRESS: You're very fat.

PROFESSOR: I think we should discuss this in the lobby.

The PROFESSOR *opens the door. The* HEAVY *closes it.*

Oh wey.

ACTRESS: Oh God.

SENATOR: I told you we had business first. I have here a warrant issued by the Department of Defence authorising me to search your room and belongings for any material or artifact that might be deemed harmful to the security of the United States of America. And this here's a warrant to confiscate any such material under the State Protection Act of 1894.

He begins to search the room.

ACTRESS: Why don't you stop him?

PROFESSOR: Please don't get involved.

ACTRESS: I am involved.

PROFESSOR: She's not.

ACTRESS: I demand to know what's going on! Why are you doing this?

SENATOR: Now that is a question the Professor hasn't thought to ask.

ACTRESS: Then ask him. Then I'll ask him! Why are you doing this?

SENATOR: It's very simple. The Atomic Energy Commission comes under review by congress next month. Another few bright young senators are going to try again to put the lid on the Nevada tests, in spite of the fact that we have to match the Soviet initiative. The President needs to be backed by top men. You're the top man.

PROFESSOR: There are a dozen others far more advanced in that field than I.

SENATOR: Who the hell's heard of them?

ACTRESS: I have. Teller, Oppenheimer.

SENATOR: Oppenheimer's name casts a shadow of doom since Nagasaki, besides why pass the buck when you can chuck it to the end of the line? There's no shadow on the pristine world of theory, no strains of Armageddon in $E = Mc^2$, even if Mc^2 does equal one hell of a big bang. Where is it?

ACTRESS: What does he want? What do you want?

SENATOR: Just a bunch of stuff that was lying around here.

ACTRESS: He wants your work? But that's not subversive.

SENATOR: Keeps it mighty close though.

ACTRESS: Because it's priceless, not secret! This is some sort of plot!

SENATOR: One thing I've learned about Communists is they think everything's a plot. You give them a parking ticket and they think it's a plot. Best way to catch a Communist is to give them three tickets in a row and if they start picking up the phone listening for taps you know you got one.

ACTRESS: How do you know if they pick up the phone?

SENATOR: You tap it! They ain't paranoid, they's communist.

PROFESSOR: Room 209. On the bed.

ACTRESS: Now hold on. If you take it you'll check the work and return it. It will be returned, won't it?

SENATOR: Well, these things take time.

ACTRESS: But there are no copies. I mean you are acting officially, aren't you?

SENATOR: Well good grief, if I wasn't there'd be nothing to stop me destroying the stuff altogether now would there?

ACTRESS: You don't suspect him of anything at all. It's just blackmail. And you just stand there. Report him.

She lifts the phone and offers it to the PROFESSOR.

SENATOR: Who to?

ACTRESS: CIA. FBI. I don't care, NBC! What's to stop us?

SENATOR: Common sense I should think. A little adverse publicity might not do a girl like you any harm, but think of the Professor's position.

PROFESSOR: I'll fetch it.

ACTRESS: No! He's just a hoodlum. He has no sense of priorities, don't trust him. Do what he wants, swear black's white, but don't risk your work.

PROFESSOR: My work is nothing.

ACTRESS: Your work is priceless!

The PROFESSOR *leaves. The* SENATOR *nods to the* HEAVY *to follow.*

SENATOR: Follow him. Meet me in the lobby.

ACTRESS: Who are you?

SENATOR: I'm a julep-drinking, nigger-whipping Louisiana boy. This isn't a game. We're talking about the survival of the free world. We do need his support.

ACTRESS: And for that you'd steal his soul?

SENATOR: Ain't difficult once you've sold your own. My orders are to find his work, take it and sit on it. Then I get a call and I hand it back or I shred the damn thing.

ACTRESS: Do you realise what it is you're talking about? It isn't just the culmination of a man's life-work although Lord knows

. . . It's a set of calculations that come close to describing the shape of Space-Time. If you'd just let him finish he'll have calculated how it all fits. How everything is. Doesn't that strike you as important?

SENATOR: You ain't talking to green-corn you know. I've given the importance of those documents a great deal of thought and I came to the conclusion that the shape of Space-Time is of fuck-all importance to any of us. It's just paper, otherwise why would he throw it all away?

ACTRESS: He trusts you.

SENATOR: Nobody's that dumb.

ACTRESS: He's weak.

SENATOR: Well, it's a dog-eat-dog world.

He finds a wad of gum on the arm of his chair that sticks to his hand.

Shit.

ACTRESS: Please, don't destroy it.

SENATOR: You know it's uncanny, at times you er . . . you've really studied the lady, ain't you?

ACTRESS: I could let you have money.

SENATOR: You trying to bribe a US Senator?

ACTRESS: Yes.

SENATOR: Takes a lot of dollars to buy a man. Where'd a girl like you get money like that?

ACTRESS: I'm not a girl.

SENATOR: I was being polite. Well you've tried appealing to my back pocket and to my intelligence. You got any more little persuasions you want to try?

ACTRESS: Maybe.

SENATOR: I beg your pardon. What was that?

ACTRESS: All right.

SENATOR: Do I understand you correctly? In return for my leaving you the calculus you're offering me sexual favours?

ACTRESS: A sexual favour. After all it's not me is it? It's her you want. Come here.

He doesn't move. She crosses to the door

and locks it, then kneels on the bed in front of him. She undoes his pants. He looks at his watch.

He hits her.
He hits her expertly, using his arms so as not to bruise. One blow to the head, one to the belly. She is thrown back across the bed.

She crawls into bed and lies there, silent, saddened, her face expressionless.
The SENATOR unlocks the door.

SENATOR: I ain't ever paid for it in my life, least of all with my integrity. Did I hurt you?

He goes to the window for air.

My son had her picture on his wall! I whipped his ass! They call her a goddam goddess, shit! She's mortal ain't she? I mean she only got where she is same way as you. Listen, you gotta look after your little body. Your little body ain't worth no pile of paper.

The door rattles.

If I hurt you I apologise. Nothing personal.

The door opens. The BALLPLAYER enters.

Well if it's not the bighitter himself!

BALLPLAYER: I don't believe it! Everytime I turn my back there's a different man in your room. Who is this?

SENATOR: Your wife's . . . Oh shit!

BALLPLAYER: Is he OK, honey?

SENATOR: It's an honour to meet you. I've been a fan for years.

ACTRESS: Sweetheart . . .

SENATOR: Game just hasn't been the same without you.

ACTRESS: Don't let him leave.

The SENATOR has been backing out. Now he hesitates, then makes for the door. The BALLPLAYER runs across and blocks it.

BALLPLAYER: Something happen while I was out?

SENATOR: Nothing at all.

BALLPLAYER: Honey?

ACTRESS: No.

BALLPLAYER: You sure?

ACTRESS: Oh God. (*She curls up and cuts herself off.*)

BALLPLAYER: Baby, what do you want me to do? Baby?

He crosses, concerned. The SENATOR moves to the door.

Hey! Sit down.

SENATOR: Look, I simply came to speak to the Professor, whose room this is, as he'll tell you . . .

BALLPLAYER: Listen, my wife asked me to keep you here. Until I find out why your choice is to sit down unaided or lie down with assistance.

SENATOR: Are you threatening me?

BALLPLAYER: No, I have never had to hit an intelligent man.

The SENATOR considers, then sits.
Enter the PROFESSOR with the calculus.

Who's he? She don't want him to leave.

The PROFESSOR ties a cord around the calculus and hands it to the SENATOR. The ACTRESS groans. She takes a sharp breath.

PROFESSOR: Now please, go away.

SENATOR: It'd be a pleasure.

BALLPLAYER: Get your butt back in the chair! She may be crazy most of the time, but she don't ask for much.

SENATOR: Can you talk some sense into this man?

PROFESSOR: I'm told it's not possible.

SENATOR: Listen, we're all civilised human beings . . .

BALLPLAYER: Baby? You want me to keep this man here? What'd he do, honey?

Her eyes meet the SENATOR's. She closes her eyes and buries her head again.

PROFESSOR: He did nothing, I promise you. His business was with me. Please, let him go.

BALLPLAYER: Honey?

ACTRESS: Let him go. All of you go.

BALLPLAYER: You a man of honour?

SENATOR: I'm a gentleman and a solipsist.

BALLPLAYER: What's a solipsist? Remind me.

SENATOR: I believe that only I exist. All the rest of you exist only in my imagination.

BALLPLAYER: That's stupid. I exist.

SENATOR: Sure you do, but only in my head.

BALLPLAYER: Bullshit. If we don't exist how come we were here before him?

SENATOR: You weren't.

BALLPLAYER: We was here before you arrived even.

SENATOR: Prove it.

BALLPLAYER: If I don't exist how come I'm arguing?

SENATOR: I like to argue.

BALLPLAYER: Wait there.

He goes out and closes the door behind him.

(*Off*:) You there?

SENATOR: Of course.

BALLPLAYER (*off*): Right, let me tell you something. I ain't with you and I still exist.

SENATOR: Prove it.

The door half opens.

BALLPLAYER: Oh no.

The door closes.

SENATOR: You're nothing.

BALLPLAYER (*off*): No I ain't.

SENATOR: Yes you are.

BALLPLAYER: Then what am I doing now? If I'm in your imagination you should be able to tell me what I'm doing.

SENATOR: Swinging an imaginary baseball bat.

BALLPLAYER (*enters*): How the fuck you know that? I do thousands of things when you ain't around. I drink coffee, I screw about, I go to movies.

SENATOR: No you don't, I only think you do.

BALLPLAYER: What about everyone else?

SENATOR: All in here.

BALLPLAYER: What about everyone who lived before you, everyone who's dead?

SENATOR: I killed them. Now remember, you all be on your best behaviour now. The folk like to think they're in the hands of gods. That's why I dreamed up you special people.

He closes the door behind him.

BALLPLAYER: I'm still here! I can hold my own intellectually. I just have to concentrate.

The ACTRESS *stirs.*

BALLPLAYER: Baby? Can you talk?

ACTRESS: Of course I can talk.

BALLPLAYER: You better honey? Did you wonder where I was? I went for a long walk and I had a good think. I finally decided what's best for me to do.

ACTRESS: You lost your work.

PROFESSOR: And I have lost my shoes.

ACTRESS: You let him walk all over you.

PROFESSOR: I have no shoes!

ACTRESS: Two-o-nine.

PROFESSOR: Ah. (*He leaves, barefoot.*)

BALLPLAYER: I got it all figured out. I had a long walk. You want a kid. I want a kid. We get on most of the time but the problem is most of the time you can't stand me, right? And why can't you stand me? Because I'm stupid. I admit it. I'm proud of it but it drives you nuts. Well let me reveal to you a secret; I am not genuinely stupid, I just enjoy being stupid. I have always enjoyed being stupid. From an early age I have revelled in stupidity. Let me tell you another thing, I am also as stubborn as a mule which explains why when you told me so often to smarten up and left books on the TV accidentally I'd never even read the ones that looked kind of interesting. But I took a walk and I had a long think. I've been thinking and what I've decided is that if you still want me to smarten up, well I reckon you're worth it. (*Pause.*) So what I reckon is while you finish your movies I'll sit right down and read a few good books. You can quiz me. And I'll get rid of the TV so there's no more TV and no more TV dinners. If you like, no more ball games. You come home. I'll smarten up. We'll have a couple of kids. No more gum.

He removes his gum and sticks it somewhere.

ACTRESS: Honey, it's over. You'd better call up your lawyer friend.

BALLPLAYER: You think so?

ACTRESS: Yeh.

BALLPLAYER: Yeh, I think so too. Maybe I'm that smart. You want some advice? You got to work out what you want.

ACTRESS: I don't want you.

BALLPLAYER: What do you want?

ACTRESS: I don't want to want.

BALLPLAYER: Yeh, but what do you want?

She weeps, or comes close to it, but stops him going to her.

ACTRESS: I want to go, do you understand? I want to go.

The BALLPLAYER tries to leave. He retrieves his gum and opens a fresh pack.

BALLPLAYER: Want some gum?

ACTRESS: I don't chew gum.

BALLPLAYER: Oh, yeah.

He looks at the card and throws it away.

He leaves.
The ACTRESS *breathes deeply and braces herself.*

She finds a box of tissues, takes a handful beneath the bedclothes and puts them into herself. She throws back the clothes.

She has been bleeding. Her slip is wet, the bedclothes stained red.

She gets up, covers the stain carefully, picks up her dress and shoes, and walks unsteadily into the bathroom, shoes in her hand.

The PROFESSOR enters, shoes in hand.

PROFESSOR: Hello?

A noise from the bathroom.
He sits with his pad but gets nowhere.

I think I might have annoyed you. I want to explain. Have you ever met a Cherokee? I met a Cherokee. It was at Harvard Observatory, in the driveway, he was collecting garbage. He said to me, I know you! You are Cherokee! I am garbage man now. You are Cherokee. Then he explained to me that to be a Cherokee you had to believe yourself to be in the centre of the universe. All true Cherokees believe this. He was a very old man. His sleeve smelled of ketchup. He told me that once he had understood his world; his life when a young man had been a prairie life; he had understood the droughts, the gods, the buffalo, but all he knew now was his dustcart, his paychecks, a one room apartment and a TV to watch. He said he no longer understood; he was no longer at the centre. No longer Cherokee. But, he said, he had heard of my head, of my thoughts like sky; he had seen me on TV. He said You are Cherokee! A young colleague of mine was there. He said not yet, not quite yet had I gotten to the centre of the universe. He meant I had not yet unified the fields, finished my work. But, said my proud colleague to that depressed Indian, just give him another eighteen months and he'll be slap bang in the middle.

Pause.

I don't want to be at the centre of my universe, their universe, or anything, of anything at all!

She enters, pristine.

ACTRESS: I think you're pathetic. The truth is you don't give a damn about your work, about people or anything else. You're so afraid of any inconvenience you didn't even object when he took away the most precious thing you ever had. You think it was yours to give away? Something that valuable isn't yours, it's everyone's. It was ours and you let it be destroyed. Aren't you ashamed? The only copy!

PROFESSOR: The fifth copy.

ACTRESS: What?

PROFESSOR: The fifth.

ACTRESS: You have copies?

PROFESSOR: No. I have destroyed four copies. Perhaps the fifth will somewhere be kept safe.

ACTRESS: I'm not following you.

PROFESSOR: I have finished my work four times. Each time I have destroyed the calculus and started over. I remember a little more this time than last but there is so much mechanical calculus I forget most of what I did before. So I do the work and then I burn the work. Four times now.

ACTRESS: But if you studied it you'd know how it all works, how it all fits. You'd know everything.

PROFESSOR: I am seventy years old. I wouldn't survive the publicity. I want to die quietly where I can just slip off the edge of this dreary, painful world. Like Columbus never did. Unfortunately. What was it your husband said? If Columbus had slipped up we'd all still be Indians. Cherokee. Instead, what are we? Americans. And listen to us. 'I am a Texan', 'I am a New Yorker', 'I am a Democrat', 'I own three automobiles'. All pathetic little beliefs fuelled by the fear of being nothing at all. And what is worse, their property, their reputations, their nations are not enough. And so they erect false gods at some supposed centre from which to measure their own position in this madman's scheme of things. She is the most beautiful, I am this beautiful. He is the most knowledgeable, I am this much knowledgeable. He is the most powerful, I am hardly powerful at all. They will not take responsibility for their world. They would load it onto the shoulders of a few. And the weight of so many people's worlds I tell you, it's too heavy!

ACTRESS: So you've stopped working?

PROFESSOR: On the contrary, I keep myself occupied. Mathematics is a splendid waste of time. I get to the end, I forgot the beginning, I go back.

ACTRESS: That's awful.

PROFESSOR: I suppose it is.

ACTRESS: It's dreadful. What are you hiding from?

PROFESSOR: I told you. Why should I stand in the centre of my universe when all around me . . .

ACTRESS: Look, would you stop talking so goddam smart! It just sounds like words. I've heard enough words! I came here to know you and all you've done is hide behind words. Now what are you hiding from?

PROFESSOR: Nothing.

ACTRESS: Don't lie to me.

PROFESSOR: Listen . . .

ACTRESS: What are you afraid of?

PROFESSOR: Nothing.

ACTRESS: Liar! What are you afraid of? Tell me.

PROFESSOR: There's something . . .

ACTRESS: What?

PROFESSOR: A thought.

ACTRESS: Tell me!

PROFESSOR: No.

ACTRESS: Please.

PROFESSOR: We burned children.

ACTRESS: Oh. But you're not responsible.

PROFESSOR: I am as responsible . . .

ACTRESS: No! You don't believe that. You didn't invent that. Tell me the truth.

Pause.

PROFESSOR: There's something worse.

ACTRESS: What could be worse?

PROFESSOR: I don't know! And I must not think about it!

Pause. She puts on her coat.

ACTRESS: Look. It's over. They won't use those things again. They've said they never will. Besides, the fat fingers on the buttons belong to the people who own the stuff that would get blown to blazes. It's what you'd call economically unviable. Unless of course they could blow up all the people and leave the cities standing, which they can't. I have to go. You want to hear my lines?

The PROFESSOR *stands, thinking.*
There is an enormous explosion. White
light hits the window.
The PROFESSOR *is silhouetted, his hair*
wild in a great wind.
The noise of the explosion stops as
suddenly as it started; it was merely a
thought.
The ACTRESS *picks up her script.*

I take a potroast from the oven, I hear the
doorbell, I run across the apartment
removing my apron, I kiss the man . . . I
disappear. No words.

Methuen New Theatrescripts

*Published in the Royal Court Writers Series
†Published in the RSC Playtexts Series
††Published in the Women's Playhouse Plays Series

SAMBA
by Michael Abbensetts

EAST-WEST & IS UNCLE JACK A
 CONFORMIST?
by Andrey Amalrik

*BURIED INSIDE EXTRA
by Thomas Babe

*THE LUCKY CHANCE
by Aphra Behn

DEREK & CHORUSES FROM AFTER
 THE ASSASSINATIONS
HUMAN CANNON
THE WAR PLAYS
by Edward Bond

SORE THROATS & SONNETS OF LOVE
 AND OPPOSITION
*THE GENIUS
by Howard Brenton

THIRTEENTH NIGHT & A SHORT
 SHARP SHOCK!
by Howard Brenton (*A Short Sharp
 Shock!* written with Tony Howard)

SLEEPING POLICEMEN
by Howard Brenton and Tunde Ikoli

†MOLIÈRE
by Mikhail Bulgakov (in a version by
 Dusty Hughes)

†MONEY
by Edward Bulwer-Lytton

RETURN TO THE FORBIDDEN PLANET
by Bob Carlton

*THE SEAGULL
by Anton Chekov (in a version by
 Thomas Kilroy)

FEN
SOFT COPS
by Caryl Churchill

SHONA, LUNCH GIRLS, THE SHELTER
by Tony Craze, Ron Hart, Johnnie
 Quarrell

WRECKERS
TEENDREAMS
by David Edgar

*MASTERPIECES
by Sarah Daniels

†THE BODY
by Nick Darke

 TORCH SONG TRILOGY
by Harvey Fierstein

†OUR FRIENDS IN THE NORTH
by Peter Flannery

RUMBLINGS
by Peter Gibbs

*OTHER WORLDS
TODAY
*THE OVERGROWN PATH
by Robert Holman

*RAT IN THE SKULL
by Ron Hutchinson

†PEER GYNT
by Henrik Ibsen (translated by David
 Rudkin)

*INSIGNIFICANCE
*CRIES FROM THE MAMMAL HOUSE
by Terry Johnson

FROZEN ASSETS
SUS
BASTARD ANGEL
BETTER TIMES
by Barrie Keeffe

UP FOR NONE & COMING APART
(Mick Mahoney & Melissa Murray)
Edited by Barrie Keeffe

*NOT QUITE JERUSALEM
by Paul Kember

*BORDERLINE
by Hanif Kureishi

TOUCHED
*TIBETAN INROADS
THE RAGGED TROUSERED
 PHILANTHROPISTS
MOVING PICTURES: Four Plays
 (*Moving Pictures; Seachange; Stars;
 Strive)*
by Stephen Lowe

PROGRESS & HARD FEELINGS
by Doug Lucie

THE PLOUGHMAN'S LUNCH
by Ian McEwan

LAVENDER BLUE & NOLI ME
TANGERE
by John Mackendrick

THICK AS THIEVES
WELCOME HOME, RASPBERRY, THE
LUCKY ONES
by Tony Marchant

†A NEW WAY TO PAY OLD DEBTS
by Philip Massinger

NICE, RUM AN' COCA COLA &
WELCOME HOME JACKO
PLAY MAS, INDEPENDENCE &
MEETINGS
by Mustapha Matura

LUNATIC AND LOVER
by Michael Meyer

*OPERATION BAD APPLE
*AN HONOURABLE TRADE
by G.F.Newman

SALONIKA
REAL ESTATE
by Louise Page

ONE FOR THE ROAD
by Harold Pinter

STRAWBERRY FIELDS
SHOUT ACROSS THE RIVER
AMERICAN DAYS
THE SUMMER PARTY
FAVOURITE NIGHTS &
CAUGHT ON A TRAIN
RUNNERS & SOFT TARGETS
BREAKING THE SILENCE
by Stephen Poliakoff

BRIMSTONE AND TREACLE
by Dennis Potter

†THE TIME OF YOUR LIFE
by William Saroyan

††SPELL NUMBER 7
by Ntozake Shange

*AUNT DAN AND LEMON
MY DINNER WITH ANDRÉ &
MARIE AND BRUCE
by Wallace Shawn (*My Dinner with André*
written with André Gregory)

LIVE THEATRE: Four Plays for Young
People
by C.P.Taylor

BAZAAR & RUMMAGE, GROPING FOR
WORDS & WOMBERANG
*THE GREAT CELESTIAL COW
THE SECRET DIARY OF ADRIAN MOLE
AGED 13¾: THE PLAY
by Sue Townsend

PLAYS BY WOMEN VOL ONE
(*Vinegar Tom* by Caryl Churchill; *Dusa,
Fish, Stas and Vi* by Pam Gems; *Tissue*
by Louise Page; *Aurora Leigh* by
Michelene Wandor)

PLAYS BY WOMEN VOL TWO
(*Rites* by Maureen Duffy; *Letters Home* by
Rose Leiman Goldemberg; *Trafford
Tanzi* by Claire Luckham; *Find Me* by
Olwen Wymark)

PLAYS BY WOMEN VOL THREE
(*Aunt Mary* by Pam Gems; *Red Devils* by
Debbie Horsfield; *Blood Relations* by
Sharon Pollock; *Time Pieces* by Lou
Wakefield and The Women's Theatre
Group

PLAYS BY WOMEN VOL FOUR
(*Objections to Sex and Violence* by
Caryl Churchill; *Rose's Story* by Grace
Daley; *Blood and Ice* by Liz Lochhead;
Pinball by Alison Lyssa)
by Michelene Wandor (Ed.)

†CLAY
by Peter Whelan

THE NINE NIGHT & RITUAL BY WATER
by Edgar White

RENTS
LENT
by Michael Wilcox

GAY PLAYS
(*Submariners* by Tom McClenaghan; *The
Green Bay Tree* by Mordaunt Shairp;
Passing By by Martin Sherman;
Accounts by Michael Wilcox)
by Michael Wilcox (Ed.)

SUGAR AND SPICE & TRIAL RUN
W.C.P.C.
by Nigel Williams

*THE GRASS WIDOW
by Snoo Wilson

HAS 'WASHINGTON' LEGS & DINGO
by Charles Wood

CUSTOM OF THE COUNTRY
THE DESERT AIR
by Nicholas Wright